THE ULTIMATE MEDITERRANEAN RECIPES COOKBOOK.

Unlocking The Hidden Fast And Easy Mediterranean Meals With 20 Delicious Recipes For Men And Women.

Sarah J. Edward

Table Of Content

INTRODUCTION

Amidst the chaotic frenzy of modern life, Elena discovered solace in the pages of the "Ultimate Mediterranean Recipes Cookbook". Its powerful allure lay not only in its sumptuous dishes but also in the transformative benefits it offered.

Guided by the cookbook, Elena embarked on a culinary journey that transcended her kitchen. Each recipe, carefully crafted with Mediterranean goodness, nourished her body and soul. The abundance of fresh vegetables, fragrant herbs, and succulent seafood rejuvenated her palate and invigorated her spirit.

But the cookbook's true magic went beyond the plate. With each dish she prepared, Elena discovered a sense of connection to the timeless traditions of the Mediterranean. From shared meals with loved ones to lively gatherings, the cookbook fostered a sense of community and brought people together.

Through the power of its flavors and the joy of its gatherings, the Ultimate Mediterranean Recipes Cookbook became a catalyst for change. It transformed Elena's life, revitalizing her health, reigniting her passion for cooking, and reminding her of the simple pleasures that make life extraordinary.

Unlocking the Secrets of THE "ULTIMATE MEDITERRANEAN RECIPES COOKBOOK "

In a coastal village, Sofia unearthed "THE ULTIMATE MEDITERRANEAN RECIPES COOKBOOK ". Its pages revealed a world of vibrant flavors and ancient traditions. Intrigued, Sofia immersed herself in the art of simplicity, the harmony of ingredients, and the magic of "The Ultimate Mediterranean Recipes Cookbook ". Guided by the book, she embarked on a culinary journey, embracing the simplicity and harmony of ingredients. As she cooked, her palate danced with the symphony of flavors, transporting her to sun-soaked shores. But it was the shared meals and heartfelt connections that truly enchanted Sofia. "The Ultimate Mediterranean Recipes Cookbook" became her language of love, celebrating life and bringing joy to every table. Through this culinary treasure, she unlocked the secrets that nourished both body and soul.

DELICIOUS MEDITERRANEAN RECIPES.

1. Greek Salad.

Ingredients:

- ❖ 2 tomatoes, diced
- ❖ 1 cucumber, sliced
- ❖ 1 red onion, thinly sliced
- ❖ 1 green bell pepper, chopped
- ❖ 200g feta cheese, crumbled
- ❖ 100g Kalamata olives
- ❖ 2 tablespoons olive oil
- ❖ 1 tablespoon red wine vinegar
- ❖ Salt and pepper to taste

Preparation:

1. In a large bowl, combine tomatoes, cucumber, onion, bell pepper, feta cheese, and olives.
2. In a small bowl, whisk together olive oil, vinegar, salt, and pepper.
3. Pour the dressing over the salad and toss gently to combine.
4. Serve chilled.

2. Tzatziki.

Ingredients:

- ❖ 1 cup Greek yogurt
- ❖ 1 cucumber, grated and drained
- ❖ 2 cloves garlic, minced
- ❖ 1 tablespoon fresh dill, chopped
- ❖ 1 tablespoon lemon juice
- ❖ Salt and pepper to taste

Preparation:

1. In a bowl, combine Greek yogurt, grated cucumber, minced garlic, dill, and lemon juice.
2. Season with salt and pepper, and mix well.
3. Before serving, place in the fridge for at least one hour

3. Spanakopita(Greek Spinach Pie)

Ingredients:

- ❖ 1 package phyllo dough
- ❖ 500g spinach, cooked and chopped
- ❖ 200g feta cheese, crumbled
- ❖ 1 onion, chopped
- ❖ 3 tablespoons olive oil
- ❖ 2 eggs, beaten
- ❖ Salt and pepper to taste

Preparation:

1. Set the oven's temperature to 180 C (350 F).
2. Heat olive oil in a pan, add chopped onion, and sauté until translucent.
3. In a bowl, combine cooked spinach, crumbled feta cheese, sautéed onion, eggs, salt, and pepper.
4. Grease a baking dish and layer phyllo dough, brushing each layer with olive oil.
5. Spread the spinach mixture evenly over the phyllo dough.
6. Top with more layers of phyllo dough, brushing each layer with olive oil.
7. To achieve golden brown results, bake for 30-35 minutes.
8. Before cutting and serving, give it a little time to chill.

4. Baba Ganoush.

Ingredients:

- ❖ 2 eggplants
- ❖ 2 cloves garlic, minced
- ❖ 2 tablespoons tahini
- ❖ 2 tablespoons lemon juice
- ❖ 2 tablespoons olive oil
- ❖ Salt and pepper to taste
- ❖ Chopped parsley for garnish

Preparation:

1. Set the oven's temperature to 200 C (400 F).
2. Place the eggplants on a baking sheet and pierce them with a fork.
3. Roast the eggplants in the oven for 30-40 minutes or until they are soft and the skin is charred.
4. The eggplants should be taken out of the oven and allowed to cool.
5. Peel off the skin and chop the flesh.
6. In a bowl, combine the chopped eggplant, minced garlic, tahini, lemon juice, olive oil, salt, and pepper.
7. Mix thoroughly until the mixture is creamy and smooth.
8. Before serving, add some chopped parsley as a garnish.

5. Moussaka.

Ingredients:

- ❖ 500g ground lamb or beef
- ❖ 2 eggplants, sliced
- ❖ 2 potatoes, sliced
- ❖ 1 onion, chopped
- ❖ 2 cloves garlic, minced
- ❖ 400g canned diced tomatoes
- ❖ 2 tablespoons tomato paste
- ❖ 1 teaspoon dried oregano
- ❖ 1 teaspoon dried thyme
- ❖ 1 teaspoon ground cinnamon
- ❖ 2 tablespoons olive oil
- ❖ Salt and pepper to taste
- ❖ Béchamel sauce (see recipe below)

Preparation:

1. Set the oven's temperature to 180 C (350 F).
2. Heat olive oil in a pan, add chopped onion and minced garlic, and sauté until translucent.
3. Cook the ground lamb or beef until browned.
4. Stir in diced tomatoes, tomato paste, dried oregano, dried thyme, ground cinnamon, salt, and pepper.
5. Remove from heat after 10 minutes of simmering.
6. In a greased baking dish, layer sliced eggplants and potatoes.
7. Spoon the meat mixture over the sliced vegetables.
8. Repeat the layers until all ingredients are used, finishing with a layer of sliced vegetables.
9. Pour the béchamel sauce over the top.
10. 40~45 minutes in the oven, or until golden brown.
11. Before serving, give the food some time to cool.

6. Béchamel Sauce.

Ingredients:

- ❖ 4 tablespoons butter
- ❖ 4 tablespoons all-purpose flour
- ❖ 2 cups milk
- ❖ Salt and pepper to taste
- ❖ A pinch of nutmeg (optional)

Preparation:

1. Over a medium heat, let the butter in a pan melt.
2. Add the flour and whisk continuously until a paste forms.
3. Add the milk gradually while continuously whisking to avoid lumps.
4. Cook the sauce over low heat, stirring frequently until it thickens.
5. Season with salt, pepper, and nutmeg (if using).
6. Reserve after removing from the heat.

7. Caprese Salad.

Ingredients:

- ❖ 2 large tomatoes, sliced
- ❖ 200g mozzarella cheese, sliced
- ❖ Fresh basil leaves
- ❖ 2 tablespoons balsamic glaze
- ❖ 2 tablespoons extra virgin olive oil
- ❖ Salt and pepper to taste

Preparation:

1. Arrange the tomato and mozzarella slices on a serving platter.
2. Tuck the fresh basil leaves in between the slices.
3. Drizzle with balsamic glaze and olive oil.
4. Season with salt and pepper.
5. Serve immediately.

8. Ratatouille.

Ingredients:

- ❖ 2 medium eggplants, diced
- ❖ 2 zucchinis, diced
- ❖ 1 red bell pepper, diced
- ❖ 1 yellow bell pepper, diced
- ❖ 1 onion, diced
- ❖ 2 cloves garlic, minced
- ❖ 400g canned diced tomatoes
- ❖ 2 tablespoons tomato paste
- ❖ 2 tablespoons olive oil
- ❖ 1 teaspoon dried thyme
- ❖ 1 teaspoon dried oregano
- ❖ Salt and pepper to taste

Preparation:

1. In a large skillet or saucepan, warm the olive oil over medium heat.
2. Add diced onion and minced garlic, and sauté until translucent.
3. Add diced eggplants, zucchinis, bell peppers, canned diced tomatoes, tomato paste, dried thyme, dried oregano, salt, and pepper.
4. All the components must be well mixed.
5. Cover the skillet or pot and simmer for 30-40 minutes, stirring occasionally, until the vegetables are tender.
6. Serve hot.

9. Greek Lemon Chicken.

Ingredients:

- ❖ 4 chicken breasts
- ❖ 4 tablespoons lemon juice
- ❖ 4 tablespoons olive oil
- ❖ 4 cloves garlic, minced
- ❖ 1 teaspoon dried oregano
- ❖ Salt and pepper to taste

<u>Preparation:</u>

1. Preheat the oven to 200°C (400°F).
2. In a bowl, combine lemon juice, olive oil, minced garlic, dried oregano, salt, and pepper.
3. Pour the marinade over the chicken breasts after placing them in a baking tray.
4. The chicken should be marinated for at least 30 minutes
5. Bake the chicken in the oven for 25-30 minutes or until cooked through.
6. Serve hot with a side of roasted vegetables or salad.

10. Tabouli (Tabbouleh)

Ingredients:

- ❖ 1 cup bulgur wheat
- ❖ 2 cups boiling water
- ❖ 1 cucumber, finely diced
- ❖ 2 tomatoes, finely diced
- ❖ Chopped fresh parsley from 1 bunch
- ❖ 1/4 cup fresh mint leaves, chopped
- ❖ 2 tablespoons lemon juice
- ❖ 2 tablespoons olive oil
- ❖ Salt and pepper to taste

1. Place the bulgur wheat in a bowl and pour boiling water over it.
2. Cover the bowl with a plate or plastic wrap and let it sit for 30 minutes.
3. Fluff the bulgur wheat with a fork and drain any excess water.
4. In a separate bowl, combine the diced cucumber, diced tomatoes, chopped parsley, chopped mint leaves, lemon juice, olive oil, salt, and pepper.
5. Add the fluffed bulgur wheat to the bowl and mix well.
6. Before serving, place in the fridge for at least one hour.

11. Shrimp Scampi.

Ingredients:

- ❖ 500g shrimp, peeled and deveined
- ❖ 4 cloves garlic, minced
- ❖ 2 tablespoons lemon juice
- ❖ 2 tablespoons butter
- ❖ 2 tablespoons olive oil
- ❖ 1/4 cup white wine
- ❖ Salt and pepper to taste
- ❖ Chopped parsley for garnish

Preparation:

1. In a large skillet, melt butter and olive oil over medium heat.
2. Once aromatic, add the minced garlic and stir.
3. Add shrimp to the skillet and cook until they turn pink, about 2-3 minutes per side.
4. Pour in lemon juice and white wine, and season with salt and pepper.
5. Cook for a further two minutes, or until the sauce begins to slightly thicken.
6. Remove from heat and garnish with chopped parsley.
7. Serve hot with crusty bread or pasta.

12. Greek Souvlaki.

Ingredients:

- ❖ 500g boneless chicken or pork, cut into cubes
- ❖ 2 tablespoons olive oil
- ❖ 2 tablespoons lemon juice
- ❖ 2 cloves garlic, minced
- ❖ 1 teaspoon dried oregano
- ❖ Salt and pepper to taste
- ❖ Skewers for grilling

Preparation:

1. In a bowl, combine olive oil, lemon juice, minced garlic, dried oregano, salt, and pepper.
2. Add the cubed chicken or pork to the marinade and toss to coat.
3. Cover the bowl and let the meat marinate in the refrigerator for at least 1 hour.
4. Heat the grill to a moderately hot setting.
5. The marinated meat is skewered using thread.
6. Grill the skewers for 10-12 minutes, turning occasionally, until the meat is cooked through and slightly charred.
7. Serve hot with pita bread and tzatziki sauce.

13. Tomato and Mozzarella Stuffed Portobello Mushrooms

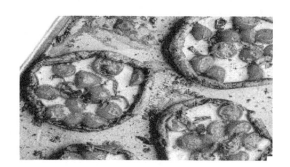

Ingredients:

- ❖ 4 large Portobello mushrooms
- ❖ 2 tomatoes, diced
- ❖ 200g mozzarella cheese, diced
- ❖ 2 cloves garlic, minced
- ❖ 2 tablespoons olive oil
- ❖ Fresh basil leaves for garnish
- ❖ Salt and pepper to taste

Preparation:

1. Preheat the oven to 200°C (400°F).
2. Remove the stems from the Portobello mushrooms and gently scrape out the gills.
3. In a bowl, combine diced tomatoes, diced mozzarella cheese, minced garlic, olive oil, salt, and pepper.
4. Spoon the tomato and mozzarella mixture into the mushroom caps.
5. Place the stuffed mushrooms on a baking sheet and bake for 15-20 minutes or until the cheese is melted and golden brown.
6. Before serving, garnish with fresh basil leaves.

14. Greek Lemon Potatoes.

Ingredients:

- ❖ 4 large potatoes, peeled and quartered
- ❖ 2 tablespoons olive oil
- ❖ 2 tablespoons lemon juice
- ❖ 2 cloves garlic, minced
- ❖ 1 teaspoon dried oregano
- ❖ Salt and pepper to taste
- ❖ For garnish, finely chopped fresh parsley

Preparation:

1. Preheat the oven to 200°C (400°F).
2. In a bowl, combine olive oil, lemon juice, minced garlic, dried oregano, salt, and pepper.
3. Add the quartered potatoes to the bowl and toss to coat.
4. Arrange the potatoes in a single layer on a greased baking dish.
5. Pour any remaining marinade over the potatoes.
6. Bake for 40-45 minutes or until the potatoes are golden brown and crispy.
7. Before serving, add freshly chopped parsley as a garnish.

15. Grilled Mediterranean Vegetables.

Ingredients:

- ❖ 2 sliced lengthwise zucchini
- ❖ 2 lengthwise sliced yellow squash
- ❖ 1 eggplant, sliced lengthwise
- ❖ 1 red bell pepper, quartered
- ❖ 1 quartered yellow bell pepper
- ❖ 1 red onion, sliced into thick rings
- ❖ 4 tablespoons olive oil
- ❖ 2 tablespoons balsamic vinegar
- ❖ 2 cloves garlic, minced
- ❖ 1 teaspoon dried thyme
- ❖ Salt and pepper to taste
- ❖ fresh parsley chopped for decoration

Preparation:

1. Set the grill's temperature to medium.
2. In a bowl, whisk together olive oil, balsamic vinegar, minced garlic, dried thyme, salt, and pepper.
3. Brush the sliced vegetables with the marinade on both sides.
4. Place the vegetables on the preheated grill and cook for 4-5 minutes per side or until tender and slightly charred.
5. Vegetables should be taken off the grill and given some time to cool.
6. Cut the grilled vegetables into bite-sized pieces.
7. Arrange the vegetables on a serving platter and garnish with chopped fresh parsley.

16. Moroccan Chicken Tagine.

Ingredients:

- ❖ 4 chicken thighs, bone-in, and skin-on
- ❖ 1 onion, sliced
- ❖ 2 cloves garlic, minced
- ❖ 2 carrots, sliced
- ❖ 1 red bell pepper, sliced
- ❖ 1 yellow bell pepper, sliced
- ❖ 400g canned diced tomatoes
- ❖ 200g canned chickpeas, drained and rinsed
- ❖ 2 tablespoons olive oil
- ❖ 2 teaspoons ground cumin
- ❖ 1 teaspoon ground cinnamon
- ❖ 1 teaspoon ground coriander
- ❖ 1 teaspoon paprika
- ❖ Salt and pepper to taste
- ❖ Chopped fresh cilantro for garnish

1. Heat olive oil in a tagine or a large pot over medium heat.
2. Add sliced onion and minced garlic, and sauté until translucent.
3. Add chicken thighs to the pot and cook until browned on all sides.
4. Add sliced carrots, sliced bell peppers, canned diced tomatoes, canned chickpeas, ground cumin, ground cinnamon, ground coriander, paprika, salt, and pepper.
5. To thoroughly incorporate all the ingredients, stir well..
6. Cover the pot and simmer for 40-45 minutes or until the chicken is cooked through and tender.
7. Add freshly cut cilantro as a garnish before serving.
8. Serve hot with couscous or rice.

17. Italian Bruschetta.

Ingredients:

- ❖ 4 slices baguette or Italian bread
- ❖ 2 ripe tomatoes, diced
- ❖ 2 cloves garlic, minced
- ❖ 2 tablespoons fresh basil, chopped
- ❖ 2 tablespoons olive oil
- ❖ Balsamic glaze for drizzling
- ❖ Salt and pepper to taste

Preparation:

1. Set the oven's temperature to 180 C (350 F).
2. Place the bread slices on a baking sheet and toast them in the oven until crispy and golden brown.
3. In a bowl, combine diced tomatoes, minced garlic, chopped fresh basil, olive oil, salt, and pepper.
4. Spoon the tomato mixture over the toasted bread slices.
5. Drizzle balsamic glaze over the top.
6. Serve immediately.

18. Greek Spanakopita.

Ingredients:

- ❖ 1 package phyllo dough
- ❖ 300g spinach, chopped
- ❖ 200g feta cheese, crumbled
- ❖ 1 onion, chopped
- ❖ 2 cloves garlic, minced
- ❖ 2 tablespoons olive oil
- ❖ 2 eggs, beaten
- ❖ Salt and pepper to taste
- ❖ Melted butter for brushing

Preparation:

1. Set the oven's temperature to 180 C (350 F).
2. Heat olive oil in a pan, add chopped onion and minced garlic, and sauté until translucent.
3. Add chopped spinach to the pan and cook until wilted.
4. Remove the pan from heat and let the spinach mixture cool.
5. In a bowl, combine cooked spinach, crumbled feta cheese, beaten eggs, salt, and pepper.
6. Melted butter should be used to brush a baking dish.
7. Layer half of the phyllo dough sheets in the baking dish, brushing each sheet with melted butter.
8. Spread the spinach and feta mixture over the phyllo dough.
9. Layer the remaining phyllo dough sheets on top, brushing each sheet with melted butter.
10. Brush melted butter on the top layer as well.
11. Bake in the oven for 30-35 minutes or until the phyllo dough is golden brown and crispy.
12. Before serving, give the food some time to cool.

19. Mediterranean Bell Peppers Stuffed.

Ingredients:

- ❖ 4 bell peppers (any color), tops removed and seeds removed
- ❖ 200g ground beef or turkey
- ❖ 1 cup cooked quinoa
- ❖ 1 onion, chopped
- ❖ 2 cloves garlic, minced
- ❖ 2 tomatoes, diced
- ❖ 1/2 cup crumbled feta cheese
- ❖ 2 tablespoons olive oil
- ❖ 1 teaspoon dried oregano
- ❖ Salt and pepper to taste

Preparation:

1. Preheat the oven to 200°C (400°F).
2. In a skillet, heat olive oil over medium heat.
3. Sauté until transparent after adding the minced garlic and onion.
4. Add ground beef or turkey to the skillet and cook until browned.
5. Stir in diced tomatoes, cooked quinoa, crumbled feta cheese, dried oregano, salt, and pepper.
6. Cook for another 2 minutes to combine all the flavors.
7. Stuff the bell peppers with the meat and quinoa mixture.
8. Place the stuffed peppers in a baking dish and bake for 25-30 minutes or until the peppers are tender.
9. Before serving, take them out of the oven and allow them to cool somewhat.

20. Tzatziki Sauce.

Ingredients:

- ❖ 1 cup Greek yogurt
- ❖ 1 cucumber, grated and squeezed to remove excess liquid
- ❖ 2 cloves garlic, minced
- ❖ 1 tablespoon lemon juice
- ❖ 1 tablespoon olive oil
- ❖ 1 tablespoon chopped fresh dill
- ❖ Salt and pepper to taste

Preparation:

1. In a bowl, combine Greek yogurt, grated cucumber, minced garlic, lemon juice, olive oil, chopped fresh dill, salt, and pepper.
2. All the components must be well mixed
3. In order for the flavors to come together, refrigerate for at least an hour
4. Serve cold as a dip or sauce with various Mediterranean dishes.

CONCLUSION

In conclusion, **"The Ultimate Mediterranean Recipes Cookbook"** is a culinary treasure trove that brings the vibrant flavors and wholesome ingredients of the Mediterranean diet right to your kitchen. With its diverse collection of 30 mouthwatering recipes, this cookbook invites you on a culinary journey through the sun-soaked landscapes and rich culinary traditions of the Mediterranean region.

From refreshing salads bursting with fresh herbs and tangy feta cheese to hearty stews simmered with aromatic spices, each recipe captures the essence of Mediterranean cuisine, emphasizing the use of wholesome ingredients like olive oil, fresh vegetables, lean proteins, and aromatic herbs.

Beyond the delectable flavors, these recipes offer a wealth of nutritional value, promoting a balanced and healthy lifestyle. Each recipe is accompanied by a detailed breakdown of the nutritional content, providing you with the essential information you need to make informed choices about your meals.

Whether you're a seasoned chef or a beginner in the kitchen, "The Ultimate Mediterranean Recipes Cookbook" is a must-have companion for anyone seeking to savor the diverse and wholesome flavors of the Mediterranean. Embrace this culinary adventure and bring the Mediterranean spirit to your dining table, one delicious recipe at a time.

COOK LIKE A PRO...

Printed in Great Britain
by Amazon

27239110R00031